TO My dearest Lisa.

FROM Chuck!

Published simultaneously in 1998 by Exley Publications Ltd in Great Britain and Exley Publications LLC in the USA.

Illustrations and anthology copyright © Lincoln Exley Designs Ltd 1998
copyright © Exley Publications Ltd 1998

12 11 10 9 8 7 6 5 4 3 2 1

ISBN 1-86187-003-5

Illustrations by Cathie Felstead.
Edited by Andrew Maxwell Hislop.
Quotations researched by Andrew Maxwell Hislop and Lincoln Exley.
Graphic Design by Acrobatix.
Concept Development by Lincoln Exley.

There is a broad range of cards and gifts featuring the artwork of Cathie Felstead produced by Lincoln Exley Designs Ltd. For further details please contact Lincoln Exley Designs, Suite 4, Kings Court, 153 High St. Watford, Hertfordshire, WD1 2ER, UK.

ACKNOWLEDGEMENTS: Lincoln Exley Designs are grateful for permission to reproduce copyright material. Whilst every effort has been made to trace copyright holders, L. E. D. would be happy to hear from any not here acknowledged. KINSLEY AMIS: From "An Ever-Fixed Mark" from *Collected Poems 1944-1979* by Kingsley Amis. © 1967 Kingsley Amis. E.E. CUMMINGS: "i like my body when it is with your" and "may I feel said he" reprinted from *Complete Poems 1904-1962,* by E.E. Cummings, ed. by George J. Firmage, by permission of W.W. Norton. © 1991 by the Trustees for the E.E. Cummings Trust and George J. Firmage. JOHNNY MERCER: From "Too Marvelous For Words". © Warner Chappell Music Inc. BRIAN PATTEN: From "Party Piece" from *Little Johnny's Confession.* Reprinted by permission of HarperCollins Publishers Ltd. BESSIE SMITH: From "Empty Bed Blues" (Part 1 and 2). © Record Music Publishing Company.

Exley Publications Ltd 16 Chalk Hill, Watford, Herts. WD1 4BN, UK.
Exley Publications LLC 232 Madison Avenue, Suite 1206, NY 10016, USA.

A Book of Hearts

A collection of words about
love featuring the illustrations
of Cathie Felstead

To Paul, love Cathie

EXLEY

NEW YORK • WATFORD UK

My true love hath my heart,
and I have his.

SIR PHILIP SIDNEY

... let there be spaces in
your togetherness,
And let the winds of the
heavens dance
between you.

KAHLIL GIBRAN

She walks in beauty, like the night
Of cloudless climes and starry skies.
LORD BYRON

Wild night!
Wild nights
Were I with thee
Wild nights should be
Our luxury.

EMILY DICKINSON

If I never met you I would have dreamed you into being.
SEBASTIAN CHANTOIX

Love conquers all things.

VIRGIL

Love is king.

MARK THORNICROFT

Love conquers all things – except poverty and toothache.

MAE WEST

How do I love thee? Let me count the ways.
I love thee to the depth and breadth and height
My soul can reach...
ELIZABETH BARRETT BROWNING

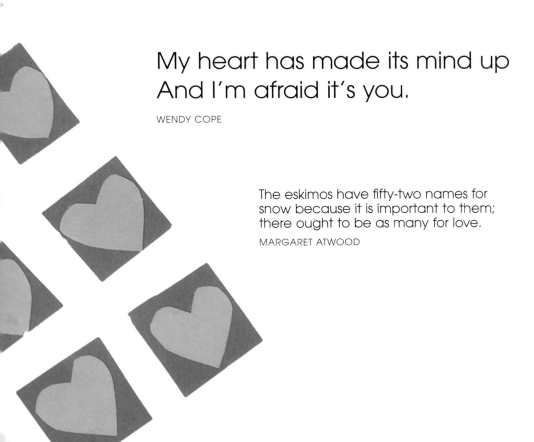

My heart has made its mind up
And I'm afraid it's you.

WENDY COPE

The eskimos have fifty-two names for
snow because it is important to them;
there ought to be as many for love.
MARGARET ATWOOD

Erotic love is the spindle on which
the earth turns.

OCTAVIO PAZ

But let's unclip our minds
And let tumble free
The mad, mangled crocodile of love.

BRIAN PATTEN

Sex is a momentary itch,
love never lets you go.

KINGSLEY AMIS

To love and to be loved is to feel the sun from both sides.

DAVID VISCOTT

Life is a flower of which love is the honey.

VICTOR HUGO

Love comforteth like the sunshine after rain.

WILLIAM SHAKESPEARE

Love's... a pardonable insanity.

SEBASTIEN CHANTOIX

One is very crazy in love.

SIGMUND FREUD

The pain of loving you is almost more than I can bear.

D H LAWRENCE

Love is an act of endless forgiveness.
PETER USTNOV

Kindness in words creates confidence. Kindness in thinking creates profoundness. Kindness in giving creates love.

LAO-TZU

The ultimate test of a relationship is to disagree but to hold hands.
ALEXANDRA PENNEY

The madness of love
is the greatest of
heaven's blessings.

PLATO

Love is something eternal – the aspect
may change, but not the essence.

VINCENT VAN GOGH

The heart that loves is always young.

PETER USTINOV

Love is the greatest refreshment in life.

PABLO PICASSO

may i feel said he
(i'll squeal said she
just once said he)
it's fun said she.

E E CUMMINGS

i like my body when it is with your
body.

E E CUMMINGS

When my bed is empty,
Makes me feel awful mean and blue.
My springs are getting rusty,
Living single like I do.

BESSIE SMITH

Love becomes the ultimate answer to the ultimate human question.

ARCHIBALD MACLEISH

If love is the answer, could
you rephrase the question.
LILY TOMLIN

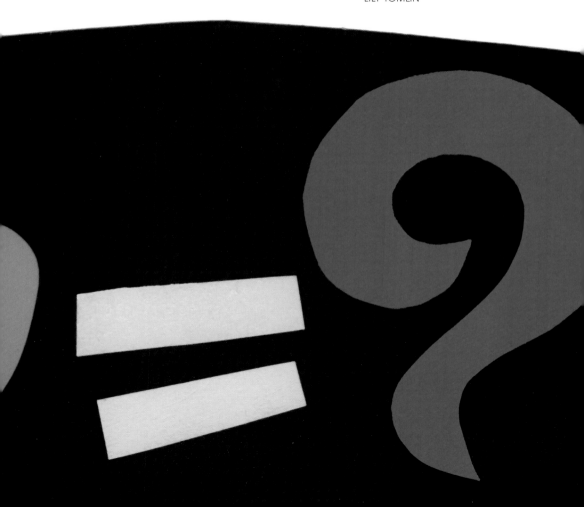

Grow old along with me!
The best is yet to be.
ROBERT BROWNING

The last of your kisses was ever the sweetest;
the last smile the brightest.
JOHN KEATS

Love is of all the passions the strongest, for it attacks simultaneously the head, the heart and the senses.

VOLTAIRE

Drink to me only with thine eyes,
And I will pledge with mine.
BEN JONSON

We know things better through love than through knowledge.

UMBERTO ECO

To love a thing means wanting it to live...

CONFUCIUS

You're much too marvelous,
Too marvelous for words.

JOHNNY MERCER

Love is something eternal,
the aspects may change,
but not the essence.

VINCENT VAN GOGH

... each day I love you more,
Today more than yesterday and less than tomorrow.

ROSEMONDE GERALD

Two human loves make one divine.

ELIZABETH BARRETT BROWNING